Fourth Book of Maccabees

By Josephus

ISBN: 978-1-63118-562-5

Christian Apocrypha Series

Other Books in this Series and Related Titles

The Book of Wisdom of Solomon by King Solomon (978-1-63118-502-1)

The Apocalypse of Peter by Peter (978-1-63118-527-4)

The Gospel of the Nativity of Mary by St. Matthew (978-1-63118-448-2)

The Vision of Saint Paul the Apostle by Paul (978-1-63118-526-7)

Early Translation of the Acts of the Apostles by Luke (978-1-63118-521-2)

The Hymn of Jesus by G. R. S. Mead (978-1-63118-409-3)

Psalms of Solomon by King Solomon (978-1-63118-439-0)

The First and Second Gospels of the Infancy of Jesus Christ (978-1-63118-415-4)

The Book of Parables by Enoch (978-1-63118-429-1)

The Testament of Abraham by Abraham (978-1-63118-441-3)

The Lives of Adam and Eve by Moses (978-1-63118-414-7)

Masonic Symbolism of King Solomon's Temple by A Mackey &c (978-1-63118-442-0)

The Secrets of Enoch by Enoch (978-1-63118-449-9)

Lost Chapters of the Book of Daniel and Related Writings (978-1-63118-417-8)

The Testament of Moses by Moses (978-1-63118-440-6)

The Book of the Watchers by Enoch (978-1-63118-416-1)

The Story of Ahikar by Ahiqar (978-1-63118-561-8)

The Odes of Solomon by King Solomon (978-1-63118-503-8)

Book of Dreams by Enoch (978-1-63118-437-6)

Kali the Mother by Sister Nivedita (978-1-63118-558-8)

The Book of Astronomical Secrets by Enoch (978-1-63118-443-7)

Audio Versions are also Available on Audible, Amazon and Apple

Other Books in this Series and Related Titles

The Hidden Mysteries of Christianity by Annie Besant (978–1–63118–534–2)

Rosicrucian Rules, Secret Signs, Codes and Symbols by various (978-1-63118-488-8)

The Hymns of Hermes by G. R. S. Mead (978-1-63118-405-5)

Freemasonry and the Egyptian Mysteries by C. W. Leadbeater (978-1-63118-456-7)

The Sepher Yetzirah and the Qabalah by M P Hall (978-1-63118-481-9)

Love and Death by Sri Aurobindo (978-1-63118-557-1)

The Historic, Mythic and Mystic Christ by Annie Besant (978–1–63118–533–5)

Masonic and Rosicrucian History by M P Hall & H Voorhis (978-1-63118-486-4)

Some Deeper Aspects of Masonic Symbolism by A E Waite (978-1-63118-461-1)

The Crest-Jewel of Wisdom by Adi Shankara (978-1-63118-475-8)

The Old Past Master by Carl H Claudy (978-1-63118-464-2)

The Influence of Pythagoras on Freemasonry and Other Essays (978-1-63118-404-8)

The Mysteries of Freemasonry & the Druids by various (978-1-63118-444-4)

Buddhist Psalms by Shinran (978-1-63118-465-9)

Catholicism, Yoga and Hinduism by Hartmann &c (978-1-63118-478-9)

Masonic Symbolism of Easter and the Christ in Masonry (978-1-63118-434-5)

Tao Te Ching & Commentary by Lao Tzu & C Johnston (978-1-63118-495-6)

Ancient Mysteries and Secret Societies by M P Hall (978-1-63118-410-9)

The Golden Verses of Pythagoras: Five Translations (978-1-63118-479-6)

Freemasonry & Catholicism by Max Heindel (978-1-63118-508-3)

A Few Masonic Sermons by A. C. Ward &c (978-1-63118-435-2)

Audio versions are also available on Audible, Amazon and Apple

Table of Contents

SERIES INTRODUCTION

The Apocrypha are a loosely knit series of books, written by early vanguards of Christianity (covering the eras of both the old and new testaments), and which comprise somewhere between about a dozen to several hundred titles, depending on whom you ask and how that person defines "Apocrypha." A small selection of these can still be found included in the Catholic bible, while a majority of the books in question, were abandoned by church officials in the early centuries of Christianity. Many of these apocryphal books were originally considered canon by early followers of Christ, in the first four centuries following his birth. It wasn't until the meeting of the Council of Nicaea in 325, that Emperor Constantine and a group of roughly 300 church bishops, gathered together with the goal of defining, standardizing and unifying an otherwise splintering Christianity, that many of these writings ceased to be included in the newly established canon. Enjoy then, this book as an example, of just one of the many books of the Christian Apocrypha, and be sure to check out other titles in this series.

INTRODUCTION

This book is like a fearful peal of thunder echoing out of the dim horrors of ancient tyranny. It is a chapter based on persecution by Antiochus, the tyrant of Syria, whom some called Epiphanes, The Madman. Roman history of the first centuries records two such tyrants--the other, Caligula, the Second Brilliant Madman.

The form of this writing is that of an oration. So carefully timed are the risings and fallings of the speech; so devastating are its arguments; so unfaltering is its logic; so deep its thrusts; so cool its reasoning--that it takes its place as a sample of the sheerest eloquence.

The keynote is--Courage. The writer begins with an impassioned statement of the Philosophy of Inspired Reason. We like to think of this twentieth Century as the Age of Reason and contrast it with the Age of Myths--yet a writing such as this is a challenge to such an assumption. We find a writer who probably belonged to the first century before the Christian Era stating a clear-cut philosophy of Reason that is just as potent today as it was two thousand years ago.

The setting of the observations in the torture chambers is unrelenting. On our modern ears attuned to gentler things it strikes appallingly. The detail's of the successive tortures (suggesting the instruments of the Spanish Inquisition centuries later) are elaborated in a way shocking to our taste. Even the emergence of the stoical characters of the Old man, the Seven Brothers, and the Mother, does nothing to soften the ferocity with which this orator conjures Courage.

The ancient Fathers of the Christian Church carefully preserved this book (we have it from a Syrian translation) as a work of high moral value and teaching, and it was undoubtedly familiar to many of the early Christian martyrs, who were aroused to the pitch of martyrdom by reading it.

CHAPTER I

An outline of philosophy from ancient times concerning Inspired Reason. Civilization has never achieved higher thought. A discussion of "Repressions." Verse 48 sums up the whole Philosophy of mankind.

PHILOSOPHICAL in the highest degree is the question I propose to discuss, namely whether the Inspired Reason is supreme ruler over the passions; and to the philosophy of it I would seriously entreat your earnest attention.

2 For not only is the subject generally necessary as a branch of knowledge, but it includes the praise of the greatest of virtues, whereby I mean self-control.

3 That is to say, if Reason is proved to control the passions adverse to temperance, gluttony and lust, it is also clearly shown to be lord over the passions, like malevolence, opposed to justice, and over those opposed to manliness, namely rage and pain and fear.

4 But, some may ask, if the Reason is master of the passions, why does it not control forgetfulness and ignorance? their object being to cast ridicule.

5 The answer is that Reason is not master over defects inhering in the mind itself, but over the passions or moral defects that are adverse to justice and manliness and temperance and judgement; and its action in their case is not to extirpate the passions, but to enable us to resist them successfully.

6 I could bring before you many examples, drawn from various sources, where Reason has proved itself master over the passions,

but the best instance by far that I can give is the noble conduct of those who died for the sake of virtue, Eleazar, and the Seven Brethren and the Mother.

7 For these all by their contempt of pains, yea, even unto death, proved that Reason rises superior to the passions.

8 I might enlarge here in praise of their virtues, they, the men with the Mother, dying on this day we celebrate for the love of moral beauty and goodness, but rather would I felicitate them on the honours they have attained.

9 For the admiration felt for their courage and endurance, not only by the world at large but by their very executioners, made them the authors of the downfall of the tyranny under which our nation lay, they defeating the tyrant by their endurance, so that through them was their country purified.

10 But I shall presently take opportunity to discuss this, after we have begun with the general theory, as I am in the habit of doing, and I will then proceed to their story, giving glory to the all-wise God.

11 Our enquiry, then, is whether the Reason is supreme master over the passions.

12 But we must define just what the Reason is and what passion is, and how many forms of passion there are, and whether the Reason is supreme over all of them.

13 Reason I take to be the mind preferring with clear deliberation the life of wisdom.

14 Wisdom I take to be the knowledge of things, divine and human, and of their causes.

15 This I take to be the culture acquired under the Law, through which we learn with due reverence the things of God and for our worldly profit the things of man.

16 Now wisdom is manifested under the forms of judgement and justice, and courage, and temperance.

17 But judgement or self-control is the one that dominates them all, for through it, in truth, Reason asserts its authority over the passions.

18 But of the passions there are two comprehensive sources, namely, pleasure and pain, and either belongs essentially also to the soul as well as to the body.

19 And with respect both to pleasure and pain there are many cases where the passions have certain sequences.

20 Thus while desire goes before pleasure, satisfaction follows after, and while fear goes before pain, after pain comes sorrow.

21 Anger, again, if a man will retrace the course of his feelings, is a passion in which are blended both pleasure and pain.

22 Under pleasure, also, comes that moral debasement which exhibits the widest variety of the passions.

23 It manifests itself in the soul as ostentation, and covetousness, and vain-glory, and contentiousness, and backbiting, and in the body as eating of strange meat, and gluttony, and gormandizing in secret.

24 Now pleasure and pain being as it were two trees, growing from body and soul, many offshoots of these passions sprout up; and each man's Reason as master-gardener, weeding and pruning and binding up, and turning on the water and directing it hither and thither, brings the thicket of dispositions and passions under domestication.

25 For while Reason is the guide of the virtues it is master of the passions.

26 Observe, now, in the first place, that Reason becomes supreme over the passions in virtue of the inhibitory action of temperance.

27 Temperance, I take it, is the repression of the desires; but of the desires some are mental and some physical, and both kinds are clearly controlled by Reason; when we are tempted towards forbidden meats, how do we come to relinquish the pleasures to be derived from them?

28 Is it not that Reason has power to repress the appetites? In my opinion it is so.

29 Accordingly when we feel a desire to eat water-animals and birds and beasts and meats of every description forbidden to us under the Law, we abstain through the predominance of Reason.

30 For the propensions of our appetites are checked and inhibited by the temperate mind, and all the movements of the body obey the bridle of Reason.

31 And what is there to be surprised at if the natural desire of the soul to enjoy the fruition of beauty is quenched?

32 This, certainly, is why we praise the virtuous Joseph, because by his Reason, with a mental effort, he checked the carnal impulse.[1] For he, a young man at the age when physical desire is strong, by his Reason quenched the impulse of his passions.

33 And Reason is proved to subdue the impulse not only of sexual desire, but of all sorts of covetings.

34 For the Law says, 'Thou shalt not covet thy neighbour's wife, nor anything that is thy neighbour's.'

35 Verily, when the Law orders us not to covet, it should, I think, confirm strongly the argument that the Reason is capable of controlling covetous desires, even as it does the passions that militate against justice.

36 How else, can a man, naturally gormandizing and greedy and drunken, be taught to change his nature, if the Reason be not manifestly the master of the passions?

37 Certainly, as soon as a man orders his life according to the Law, if he is miserly he acts contrary to his nature, and lends money

---

[1] See The Testament of Joseph, page 260.

to the needy without interest, and at the seventh-year periods cancels the debt.

38 And if he is parsimonious, he is overruled by the Law through the action of Reason, and refrains from gleaning his stubbles or picking the last grapes from his vineyards.

39 And with regard to all the rest we can recognize that Reason is in the position of master over the passions or affections.

40 For the Law ranks above affection for parents, so that a man may not for their sakes surrender his virtue, and it overrides love for a wife, so that if she transgress a man should rebuke her, and it governs love for children, so that if they are naughty a man should punish them, and it controls the claims of friendship, so that a man should reprove his friends if they do evil.

41 And do not think it a paradoxical thing when Reason through the Law is able to overcome even hatred, so that a man refrains from cutting down the enemy's orchards, and protects the property of the enemy from the spoilers, and gathers up their goods that have been scattered.

42 And the rule of Reason is likewise proved to extend through the more aggressive passions or vices, ambition, vanity, ostentation, pride, and backbiting.

43 For the temperate mind repels all these debased passions, even as it does anger, for it conquers even this.

44 Yea, Moses when he was angered against Dathan and Abiram did not give free course to his wrath, but governed his anger by his Reason.

45 For the temperate mind is able, as I said, to win the victory over the passions, modifying some, while crushing others absolutely.

46 Why else did our wise father Jacob blame the houses of Simeon and Levi for their unreasoning slaughter of the tribe of the Shechemites, saying, 'Accursed be their anger!'

47 For had not Reason possessed the power to restrain their anger he would not have spoken thus.

48 For in the day when God created man, he implanted in him his passions and inclinations, and also, at the very same time, set the mind on a throne amidst the senses to be his sacred guide in all things; and to the mind he gave the Law, by the which if a man order himself, he shall reign over a kingdom that is temperate, and just, and virtuous, and brave.

CHAPTER II

The ruling of Desire and Anger. The story of David's thirst. Stirring chapters of ancient history. Savage attempts to make the Jews eat swine. Interesting references to an ancient bank (Verse 21.)

WELL then, someone may ask, if Reason is master of the passions why is it not master of forgetfulness and ignorance?

2 But the argument is supremely ridiculous. For Reason is not shown to be master over passions or defects in itself, but over those of the body.

3 For example, none of you is able to extirpate our natural desire, but the Reason can enable him to escape being made a slave by desire.

4 None of you is able to extirpate anger from the soul, but it is possible for the Reason to come to his aid against anger.

5 None of you can extirpate a malevolent disposition, but Reason can be his powerful ally against being swayed by malevolence.

6 Reason is not the extirpate of the passions, but their antagonist.

7 The case of the thirst of King David may serve at least to make this clearer.

8 For when David had fought the live-long day against the Philistines, and by the help of our country's warriors had slain many of them, he came at eventide, all fordone with sweat and toil, to the royal tent, around which was encamped the whole army of our ancestors.

9 So all the host fell to their evening meal; but the king, being consumed with an intense thirst, though he had abundance of water, was unable to slake it.

10 Instead, an irrational desire for the water that was in the possession of the enemy with growing intensity burned him up and unmanned and consumed him.

11 Then when his body-guard murmured against the craving of the king, two youths, mighty warriors, ashamed that their king should lack his desire, put on all their armour, and took a water-vessel, and scaled the enemy's ramparts; and stealing undetected past the guards at the gate, they searched through all the enemy's camp.

12 And they bravely found the spring, and drew from it a draught for the king.

13 But David, though still burning with the thirst, considered that such a draught, reckoned as equivalent to blood, was a grievous danger to his soul.

14 Therefore, opposing his Reason to his desire, he poured out the water as an offering to God.

15 For the temperate mind is able to conquer the dictates of the passions, and to quench the fires of desire, and to wrestle victoriously with the pangs of our bodies though they be exceeding strong, and by the moral beauty and goodness of Reason to defy with scorn all the domination of the passions.

16 And now the occasion calls us to set forth the story of the self-controlled Reason.

17 At a time when our fathers enjoyed great peace through the due observance of the Law, and were in happy case, so that Seleucus Nicanor, the king of Asia, sanctioned the tax for the

temple-service, and recognized our polity, precisely then, certain men, acting factiously against the general concord, involved us in many and various calamities.

18 Onias, a man of the highest character, being then high priest and having the office for his life, a certain Simon raised a faction against him, but since despite every kind of slander he failed to injure him on account of the people, he fled abroad with intent to betray his country.

19 So he came to Apollonius, the governor of Syria and Phoenicia and Cilicia, and said, 'Being loyal to the king, I am here to inform you that in the treasuries of Jerusalem are stored many thousands of private deposits, not belonging to the temple account, and rightfully the property of King Seleucus.'

20 Apollonius having made inquiry into the details of the matter, praised Simon for his loyal service to the king, and hastening to the court of Seleucus, disclosed to him the valuable treasure; then, after receiving authority to deal with the matter, he promptly marched into our country, accompanied by the accursed Simon and a very powerful army, and announced that he was there by the king's command to take possession of the private deposits in the treasury.

21 Our people were deeply angered by this announcement, and protested strongly, considering it, an outrageous thing for those who had entrusted their deposits to the temple treasury to be robbed of them, and they threw all possible obstacles in his way.

22 Apollonius, however, with threats, made his way into the temple.

23 Then the priests in the temple and the women and children besought God to come to the rescue of his Holy Place that was being violated; and when Apollonius with his armed host

marched in to seize the moneys, there appeared from heaven angels, riding upon horses, with lightning flashing from their arms, and cast great fear and trembling upon them.

24 And Apollonius fell down half-dead in the Court of the Gentiles, and stretched out his hands to heaven, and with tears he entreated the Hebrews that they would make intercession for him and stay the wrath of the heavenly host.

25 For he said that he had sinned and was worthy even of death, and that if he were given his life he would laud to all men the blessedness of the Holy Place.

26 Moved by these words, Onias, the high-priest, although most scrupulous in other cases, made intercession for him lest king Seleucus should possibly think that Apollonius had been overthrown by a human device and not by divine justice.

27 Apollonius, accordingly, after his astonishing deliverance departed to report to the king the things that had befallen him.

28 But Seleucus dying, his successor on the throne was his son Antiochus Epiphanes, an overweening terrible man; who dismissed Onias from his sacred office, and made his brother Jason high-priest instead, the condition being that in return for the appointment Jason should pay him three thousand six hundred and sixty talents yearly.

29 So he appointed Jason high-priest and made him chief ruler over the people.

30 And he (Jason) introduced to our people a new way of life and a new constitution in utter defiance of the Law; so that not only did he lay out a gymnasium on the Mount of our fathers, but he actually abolished the service of the temple.

31 Wherefore the divine justice was kindled to anger and brought Antiochus himself as an enemy against us.

32 For when. be was carrying on war with Ptolemy in Egypt and heard that the people of Jerusalem had rejoiced exceedingly over a report of his death, he immediately marched back against them.

33 And when he had plundered the city he made a decree denouncing the penalty of death upon any who should be seen to live after the law of our fathers.

34 But he found all his decrees of no avail to break down the constancy of our people to the Law, and he beheld all his threats and penalties utterly despised, so that even women for circumcising their sons, though they knew beforehand what would be their fate, were flung, together with their offspring, headlong from the rocks.

35 When therefore his decrees continued to be contemned by the mass of the people, he personally tried to force by tortures each man separately to eat unclean meats and thus abjure the Jewish religion.

36 Accordingly, the tyrant Antiochus, accompanied by his councillors, sat in judgement on a certain high place with his troops drawn up around him in full armour, and he ordered his guards to drag there every single man of the Hebrews and compel them to eat swine's flesh and things offered to idols; but if any should refuse to defile themselves with the unclean things, they were to be tortured and put to death.

37 And when many had been taken by force, one man first from among the company was brought before Antiochus, a Hebrew whose name was Eleazar, a priest by birth, trained in knowledge of the law, a man advanced in years and well known to many of the tyrant's court for his philosophy.

38 And Antiochus, looking on him, said: 'Before I allow the tortures to begin for you, O venerable man, I would give you this counsel, that you should eat of the flesh of the swine and save your life; for I respect your age and your grey hairs, although to have worn them so long a time, and still to cling to the Jewish religion, makes me think you no philosopher.

39 For most excellent is the meat of this animal which Nature has graciously bestowed upon us, and why should you abominate it? Truly it is folly not to enjoy innocent pleasures, and it is wrong to reject Nature's favours.

40 But it will be still greater folly, I think, on your part if with idle vapouring about truth you shall proceed to defy even me to your own punishment.

41 Will you not awake from your preposterous philosophy? Will you not fling aside the nonsense of your calculations and, adopting another frame of mind befitting your mature years, learn the true philosophy of expediency, and how to my charitable counsel, and have pity on your own venerable age?

42 For consider this, too, that even if there be some Power whose eye is upon this religion of yours, he will always pardon you for a transgression done under compulsion.'

43 bus urged by the tyrant to the unlawful eating of unclean meat, Eleazar asked permission to speak; and receiving it, he began his speech before the court as follows:

44 'We, O Antiochus, having accepted the Divine Law as the Law of our country, do not believe any stronger necessity is laid upon us than that of our obedience to the Law.

45 Therefore we do surely deem it right not. in any way whatsoever to transgress the Law.

46 And yet, were our Law, as you suggest, not truly divine, while we vainly believed it to be divine, not even so would it be right for us to destroy our reputation for piety.

47 Think it not, then, a small sin for us to eat the unclean thing, for the transgression of the Law, be it in small things or in great, is equally heinous; for in either case equally the Law is despised.

48 And you scoff at our philosophy, as if under it we were living in a manner contrary to reason.

49 Not so, for the Law teaches us self-control, so that we are masters of all our pleasures and desires and are thoroughly trained in manliness so as to endure all pain with readiness; and it teaches justice, so that with all our various dispositions we act fairly, and it teaches righteousness, so that with due reverence we worship only the God who is.

50 Therefore do we eat no unclean meat; for believing our Law to be given by God, we know also that the Creator of the world, as a Lawgiver, feels for us according to our nature.

51 He has commanded us to eat the things that will be convenient for our souls, and he has forbidden us to eat meats that would be the contrary.

52 But it is the act of a tyrant that you should compel us not only to transgress the Law, but should also make us eat in such manner that you may mock at' this defilement so utterly abominable to us.

53 But you shall not mock at me thus, neither will I break the sacred oaths of my ancestors to keep the Law, not even though you tear out mine eyes and bum out mine entrails.

54 I am not so unmanned by old age but that when righteousness is at stake the strength of youth returns to my Reason.

55 So twist hard your racks and blow your furnace hotter. I do not so pity mine old age as to break the Law of my fathers in mine own person.

56 I will not belie thee, O Law that wast my teacher; I will not desert thee, O beloved self-control; I will not put thee to shame, O wisdom-loving Reason, nor will I deny ye, O venerated priesthood and knowledge of the Law.

57 Neither shalt thou sully the pure mouth of mine old age and my lifelong constancy to the Law. Clean shall my fathers receive me, unafraid of thy torments even to the death.

58 For thou indeed mayest be tyrant over unrighteous men, but thou shalt not lord it over my resolution in the matter of righteousness either by thy words or through thy deeds.'

CHAPTER III

Eleazar, the gentle spirited old man, shows such fortitude that even as we read these words 2000 years later, they seem like an inextinguishable fire.

BUT when Eleazar replied thus eloquently to the exhortations of the tyrants, the guards around him dragged him roughly to the torturing place.

2 And first they unclothed the old man, who was adorned with the beauty of holiness.

3 Then binding his arms on either side they scourged him, a herald standing and shouting out over against him, 'Obey the orders of the king!'

4 But the great-souled and noble man, an Eleazar in very truth, was no more moved in his mind than if he were being tormented in a dream; yea, the old man keeping his eyes steadfastly raised to heaven suffered his flesh to be tom by the scourges till he was bathed in blood and his sides became a mass of wounds; and even when he fell to the ground because his body could no longer support the pain he still kept his Reason erect and inflexible.

5 With his foot then one of the cruet guards as he fell kicked him savagely in the side to make him get up.

6 But he endured the anguish, and despised the compulsion, and bore up under the torments, and like a brave athlete taking punishment, the old man outwore his tormentors.

7 The sweat stood on his brow, and he drew his breath in hard gasps, till his nobility of soul extorted the admiration of his tormentors themselves.

8 Hereupon, partly in pity for his old age, partly in sympathy for their friend, partly in admiration of his courage, some of the courtiers of the king went tip to him and said:

9 'Why, O Eleazar, dost thou madly destroy thyself in this misery? We will bring to thee of the seethed meats, but do thou feign only to partake of the swine's flesh, and so save thyself.'

10 And Eleazar, as if their counsel did but add to his tortures, cried loudly: 'No. May we sons of Abraham never have so evil a thought as with faint heart to counterfeit a part unseemly to us.

11 Contrary to Reason, indeed, were it for us, after living unto the truth till old age, and guarding in lawful guise the repute of so living, now to change and become in our own persons a pattern to the young of impiety, to the end that we should encourage them to eat unclean meat.

12 Shame were it if we should live on a little longer, during that little being mocked of all men for cowardice, and while despised by the tyrant as unmanly should fail to defend the Divine Law unto the death.

13 Therefore, O sons of Abraham, do ye die nobly for righteousness' sake; but as for you, O minions of the tyrant, why pause ye in your work?'

14 So they, seeing him thus triumphant over the tortures and unmoved even by the pity of his executioners, dragged him to the fire.

15 There they cast him on it, burning him with cruelly cunning devices, and they poured broth of evil odour into his nostrils.

16 But when the fire already reached to his bones and he was about to give up the ghost, he lifted up his eyes to God and said:

17 'Thou, O God, knowest that though I might save myself I am dying by fiery torments for thy Law. Be merciful unto thy people, and let our punishment be a satisfaction in their behalf. Make my blood their purification, and take my soul to ransom their souls,,

18 And with these words the holy man nobly yielded up his spirit under the torture I and for the sake of the Law held out by his Reason even against the torments unto death.

19 Beyond question, then, the Inspired Reason is master over the passions; for if his passions or sufferings had prevailed over his Reason we should have credited them with this evidence of their superior power.

20 But now his Reason having conquered his passions, we properly attribute to it the power of commanding them.

21 And it is right that we should admit that the mastery lies with Reason, in cases at least where it conquers pains that come from outside ourselves; for it were ridiculous to deny it.

22 And my proof covers not only the superiority of Reason to pains, but its superiority to pleasures also; neither does it surrender to them.

CHAPTER IV

This so called "Age of Reason" may in this chapter read that the Philosophy of Reason is 2000 years old. The story of seven sons and their mother.

FOR the Reason of our father Eleazar, like a fine steersman steering the ship of sanctity on the sea of the passions, though buffeted by the threats of the tyrant and swept by the swelling waves of the tortures, never shifted for one moment the helm of sanctity until he sailed into the haven of victory over death.

2 No city besieged with many and cunning engines ever defended itself so well as did that holy man when his sacred soul was attacked with scourge and rack and flame, and he moved them who were laying siege to his soul through his Reason that was the shield of sanctity.

3 For our father Eleazar, setting his mind film as a beetling sea-cliff, broke the mad onset of the surges of the passions.

4 O priest worthy of thy priesthood, thou didst not defile thy holy teeth, nor didst thou befoul with unclean meat thy belly that had room only for piety and purity.

5 O confessor of the Law and philosopher of the Divine life! Such should those be whose office is to serve the Law and defend it with their own blood and honourable sweat in the face of sufferings to the death.

6 Thou, O father, didst fortify our fidelity to the Law through thy steadfastness unto glory; and having spoken in honour of holiness thou didst not belie thy speech, and didst confirm the words of divine philosophy by thy deeds, O aged man that wast more forceful than the tortures.

7 O reverend elder that wast tenser-strung than the flame, thou great king over the passions, Eleazar.

8 For as our father Aaron, armed with the censer, ran through the massed congregation against the fiery angel and overcame him, so the son of Aaron, Eleazar, being consumed by the melting heat of the fire, remained unshaken in his Reason.

9 And yet most wonderful of all, he, being an old man, with the sinews of his body unstrung and his muscles relaxed and his nerves weakened, grew a young man again in the spirit of his Reason and with Isaac-like Reason turned the hydra-headed torture to impotence.

10 O blessed age, O reverend grey head, O life faithful to the Law and perfected by the seal of death!

11 Assuredly, then, if an old man despised the torments unto death for righteousness' sake it must be admitted that the Inspired Reason is able to guide the passions.

12 But some perhaps may answer that not all men are masters of the passions because not all men have their Reason enlightened.

13 But as many as with their whole heart make righteousness their first thought, these alone are able to master the weakness of the flesh, believing that unto God they die not, as our patriarchs, Abraham and Isaac and Jacob, died not, but that they live unto God.

14 Therefore there is-nothing contradictory in certain persons appearing to be slaves to passion in consequence of the weakness of their Reason.

15 For who is there that being a philosopher following righteously the whole rule of philosophy, and having put his trust in

God, and knowing that it is a blessed thing to endure all hardness for the sake of virtue, would not conquer his passions for the sake of righteousness?

16 For the wise and self-controlled man alone is the brave ruler of the passions.

17 Yea, by this means even young boys, being philosophers by virtue of the Reason which is according to righteousness, have triumphed over yet more grievous tortures.

18 For when the tyrant found himself notably defeated in his first attempt, and impotent to compel an old man to eat unclean meat, then truly in violent rage he ordered the guards to bring others of the young men of the Hebrews, and if they would eat unclean meat to release them after eating it, but if they refused, to torture them yet more savagely.

19 And under these orders of the tyrant seven brethren together with their aged mother were brought prisoners before him, all handsome, and modest, and well-born,--and generally attractive.

20 And when the tyrant saw them there, standing as if they were a festal choir with their mother in the midst, he took notice of them, and struck by their noble and distinguished bearing he smiled at them, and calling them nearer said:

21 'O young men, I wish well to each one of you, and admire your beauty, and honour highly so large a band of brothers; so not only do I advise you not to persist in the madness of that old man who has already suffered, but I even entreat of you to yield to me and become partakers in my friendship.

22 For, as I am able to punish those who disobey my orders, so am I able to advance those who do obey me.

23 Be assured then that you shall be given positions of importance and authority in my service if you will reject the ancestral law of your polity.

24 Share in the Hellenic life, and walk in a new way, and take some pleasure in your youth; for if you drive me to anger with your disobedience you will compel me to resort to terrible penalties and put every single one of you to death by torture.

25 Have pity then on yourselves, whom even I, your opponent, pity for your youth and your beauty.

26 Will you not consider with yourselves this thing, that if you disobey me there is nothing before you but death in torments?'

27 With these words he ordered the instruments of torture to be brought forward in order to persuade them by fear to eat unclean meat.

28 But when the guards had produced wheels, and joint-dislocators, and racks, and bone-crushers, and catapults, and cauldrons, and braziers, and thumb-screws, and iron claws, and wedges, and branding irons, the tyrant spoke again and said:

29 'You had better feel fear, my lads, and the justice you worship will pardon your unwilling transgression.'

30 But they, hearing his persuasions, and seeing his dreadful engines, not only showed no fear but actually arrayed their philosophy in opposition to the tyrant, and by their right Reason did abase his tyranny.

31 And yet consider; supposing some amongst them to have been faint-hearted and cowardly, what sort of language would they have used? would it not have been to this effect?

32 'Alas! miserable creatures that we are and foolish above measure! When the king invites us and appeals to us on terms of kind treatment shall we not obey him?

33 Why do we encourage ourselves with vain desires and dare a disobedience that is to cost us our lives? Shall we not, O men my brothers, fear the dread instruments and weigh well his threats of the tortures, and abandon these empty vaunts and this fatal bragging?

34 Let us take pity on our own youth and have compassion on our mother's age; and let us lay to heart that if we disobey we shall die.

35 And even the divine justice will have mercy on us, if compelled by necessity we yield to the king in fear. Why should we cast away from us this dear life and rob ourselves of this sweet world?

36 Let us not strive against necessity nor with vain confidence invite our torture.

37 Even the Law itself does not willingly condemn us to death, we being in terror of the instruments of torture.

38 Why does such contentiousness inflame us and a fatal obstinacy find favour with us, when we might have a peaceful life by obeying the king?'

39 But no such words escaped these young men at the prospect of the torture, nor did such thoughts enter into their minds.

40 For they were despisers of the passions and masters over pain.

CHAPTER V

A chapter of horror and torture revealing ancient tyranny at its utmost savagery. Verse 26 is profound truth.

AND thus no sooner did the tyrant conclude his urging of them to eat unclean meat than all with one voice together, and as with one soul, said to him:

2 'Why dost thou delay, O tyrant? We are ready to die rather than transgress the commandments of our fathers.

3 For we should be putting our ancestors also to shame, if we did not walk in obedience to the Law and take Moses as our counsellor.

4 O tyrant that counsellest us to transgress the Law, do not, hating us, pity us beyond ourselves.

5 For we esteem thy mercy, giving. us our life in return for a breach of the Law, a thing harder to bear than death itself.

6 Thou wouldst terrify us with thy threats of death under torture, as if a little while ago thou hadst learned nothing from Eleazar.

7 But if the old men of the Hebrews endured the tortures for righteousness' sake, yea, until they died, more befittingly will we young men die despising the torments of thy compulsion, over which he our aged teacher also triumphed.

8 Make trial therefore, O tyrant. And if thou takest our lives for the sake of righteousness, think not that thou hurtest us with thy tortures.

9 For we through this our evil entreatment and our endurance of it shall win the prize of virtue; but thou for our cruel murder shalt suffer at the hands of divine justice sufficient torment by fire for ever.'

10 These words of the youths redoubled the wrath of the tyrant, not at their disobedience only but at what he considered their ingratitude.

11 So by his orders the scourgers brought forward the eldest of them and stripped him of his garment and bound his hands and arms on either side with thongs.

12 But when they had scourged him till they were weary, and gained nothing thereby, they cast him upon the wheel.

13 And on it the noble youth was racked till his bones were out of joint. And as joint after joint gave way, he denounced the tyrant in these words:

14 'O thou most abominable tyrant, thou enemy of the justice of heaven and bloody-minded, thou dost torment me in this fashion not for manslaying nor for impiety but for defending the Law of God.'

15 And when the guards said to him, 'Consent to eat, that so you may be released from your tortures,' he said to them, 'Your method, O miserable minions, is not strong enough to lead captive my Reason. Cut off my limbs, and burn my flesh, and twist my joints; through all the torments I will show you that in behalf of virtue the sons of the Hebrews alone are unconquerable.'

16 As he thus spake they set hot coals upon him besides, and intensifying the torture strained him yet tighter on the wheel.

17 And all the wheel was besmeared with his blood, and the heaped coals were quenched by the humours of his body dropping down, and the rent flesh ran round the axles of the machine.

18 And with his bodily frame already in dissolution this great-souled youth, like a true son of Abraham, groaned not at all; but as if he were suffering a change by fire to incorruption, he nobly endured the torment, saying:

19 'Follow my example, O brothers. Do not for ever desert me, and forswear not our brotherhood in nobility of soul.

20 War a holy and honourable warfare on behalf of righteousness, through which may the just Providence that watched over our fathers become merciful unto his people and take vengeance on the accursed tyrant.'

21 And with these words the holy youth yielded up the ghost.

22 But while all were wondering at his constancy of soul, the guards brought forward the second in age of the. sons, and grappling him with sharp-clawed hands of iron they fastened him to the engines and the catapult.

23 But when they heard his noble resolve in answer to their question, 'Would he eat rather than he tortured?' these panther-like beasts tore at his sinews with claws of iron, and rent away all the flesh from his cheeks, and tore off the skin from his head.

24 But he steadfastly enduring this agony said, 'How sweet is every form of death for the sake of the righteousness of our fathers!'

25 And to the tyrant he said, 'O most ruthless of tyrants, doth not it seem to thee that at this moment thou thyself sufferest tortures worse than mine in seeing thy tyranny's arrogant intention overcome by my endurance for righteousness' sake?

26 For I am supported under pain by the joys that come through virtue, whereas thou art in torment whilst glorying in thy impiety; neither shalt thou escape, O most abominable tyrant, the penalties of the divine wrath.'

27 And when he had bravely met his glorious death, the third son was brought forward and was earnestly entreated by many to taste and so to save himself.

28 But he answered in a loud voice, 'Are ye ignorant that the same father begat me and my brothers that are dead, and the same mother gave us birth, and in the same doctrines was I brought up?

29 I do not forswear the noble bond of brotherhood.

30 Therefore if ye have any engine of torment, apply it to this body of mine; for my soul ye cannot reach, not if ye would.'

31 But they were greatly angered at the bold speech of the man, and they dislocated his hands and his feet with their dislocating engines, and wrenched his limbs out of their sockets, and unstrung them; and they twisted round his fingers, and his arms, and his legs, and his elbow-joints.

32 And in no wise being able to strangle his spirit they stripped off his skin, taking the points of the fingers with it, and tore in Scythian fashion the scalp from his head, and straightway brought him to the wheel.

33 And on this they twisted his spine till he saw his own flesh hanging in strips and great gouts of blood pouring down from his entrails.

34 And at the point of death he said, 'We, O most abominable tyrant, suffer thus for our upbringing and our virtue that

are of God; but thou for thy impiety and thy cruelty shall endure torments without end.'

35 And when' this man had died worthily of his brothers, they brought up the fourth, and said to him, 'Be not thou also mad with the same madness as thy brethren, but obey the king and save thyself.'

36 But he said unto them, 'For me ye have no fire so exceeding hot as to make me a coward.

37 By the blessed death of my brethren, by the eternal doom of the tyrant, and by the glorious life of the righteous, I will not deny my noble brotherhood.

38 Invent tortures, O tyrant, in order that thou mayest learn thereby that I am brother of those who have been already tortured.'

39 When he heard this the bloodthirsty, murderous, and utterly abominable Antiochus bade them cut out his tongue.

40 But he said, 'Even if thou dost remove my organ of speech, God is a hearer also of the speechless.

41 Lo, I put out my tongue ready: cut it out, for thou shalt not thereby silence my Reason.

42 Gladly do we give our bodily members to be mutilated for the cause of God.

43 But God will speedily pursue after thee; for thou cuttest out the tongue that sang songs of praise unto him.'

44 But when this man also was put to a death of agony with the tortures, the fifth sprang forward saying, 'I shrink not, O tyrant, from demanding the torture for virtue's sake.

45 Yea, of myself I come forward, in order that, slaying me also, thou mayest by yet more misdeeds increase the penalty thou owest to the justice of Heaven.

46 O enemy of virtue and enemy of man, for what crime dost thou destroy us in this way?

47 Doth it seem evil to thee that we worship the Creator of all and live according to his virtuous Law?

48 But these things are worthy of honours not of tortures, if thou didst understand human aspirations and hadst hope of salvation before God.

49 Lo, now thou art God's enemy and makest war on those that worship God.'

50 As he spake thus the guards bound him and brought him before the catapult; and they tied him thereto on his knees, and, fastening them there with iron clamps, they wrenched his loins over the rolling 'wedge' so that he was completely curled back like a scorpion and every joint was disjointed.

51 And thus in grievous strait for breath and anguish of body he exclaimed, 'Glorious, O tyrant, glorious against thy will are the boons that thou bestowest on me, enabling me to show my fidelity to the Law through yet more honourable tortures.'

52 And when this man also was dead, the sixth was brought, a mere boy, who in answer to the tyrant's inquiry whether he was willing to eat and be released, said:

53 'I am not so old in years as my brethren, but I am as old in mind. For we were born and reared for the same purpose and are equally bound also to die for the same cause; so if thou chooseth to torture us for not eating unclean meat, torture.'

54 As he spake these words they brought him to the wheel, and with care they stretched him out and dislocated the bones of his back and set fire under him.

55 And they made sharp skewers red-hot and ran them into his back, and piercing through his sides they burned away his entrails also.

56 But he in the midst of his tortures exclaimed, 'O contest worthy of saints, wherein so many of us brethren, in the cause of righteousness, have been entered for a competition in torments, and have not been conquered!

57 For the righteous understanding, O tyrant, is unconquerable.

58 In the armour of virtue I go to join my brothers in death, and to add in myself one strong avenger more to punish thee, O deviser of the tortures and enemy of the truly righteous.

59 We six youths have overthrown thy tyranny. 'For is not thine impotence to alter our Reason or force us to eat unclean meat an overthrow for thee?

60 Thy fire is cool for us, thy engines of torture torment not, and thy violence is impotent.

61 For the guards have been officers for us, not of a tyrant, but of the Divine Law; and therefore have we our Reason yet unconquered.'

CHAPTER VI

Brotherly bonds and a mother's love.

AND when this one also died a blessed death, being cast into the cauldron, the seventh son, the youngest of them all, came forward.

2 But the tyrant, although fiercely exasperated by his brethren, felt pity for the boy, and seeing him there already bound he had him brought near, and sought to persuade him, saying: 'Thou seest the end of the folly of thy brethren; for through their disobedience they have been racked to death. Thou, too, if thou dost not obey, wilt thyself also be miserably tortured and put to death before thy time; but if thou dost obey thou shalt be my friend, and thou shalt be advanced to high office in the business of the kingdom.'

4 And while thus appealing to him he sent for the boy's mother, in order that in her sorrow for the loss of so many sons she might urge the survivor to obey and be saved.

5 But the mother, speaking in the Hebrew tongue, as I shall tell later on, encouraged the boy, and he said to the guards, 'Loose me, that I may speak to the king and to all his friends with him.'

6 And they, rejoicing at the boy's request, made haste to loose him.

7 And running up to the red-hot brazier, 'O impious tyrant,' he cried, 'and most ungodly of all sinners, art thou not ashamed to take thy blessings and thy kingship at the hands of God, and to slay his servants and torture the followers of righteousness?

8 For which things the divine justice delivers thee unto a more rapid and an eternal fire and torments which shall not leave hold on thee to all eternity.

9 Art thou not ashamed, being a man, O wretch with the heart of a wild beast, to take men of like feelings with thyself, made from the same elements, and tear out their tongues, and scourge and torture them in this manner?

10 But while they have fulfilled their righteousness towards God in their noble deaths, thou shalt miserably cry "Woe is met" for thy unjust slaying of the champions of virtue.'

11 And then standing on the brink of death he said, 'I am no renegade to the witness borne by my brethren.

12 And I call upon the God of my fathers to be merciful unto my nation.

13 And thee will he Punish both in this present life and after that thou art dead.'

14 And with this prayer he cast himself into the red-hot brazier, and so gave up the ghost.

15 If therefore the seven brethren despised the tortures even to the death, it is universally proved that the Inspired Reason is supreme lord over the passions.

16 For if they had yielded to their passions or sufferings and eaten unclean meat we should have said that they had been conquered thereby.

17 But in this cam it was not so; on the contrary by their Reason, which was commended in the sight of God, they rose superior to their passions.

18 And it is impossible to deny the supremacy of the mind; for they won the victory over their passions and their pains.

19 How can we do otherwise than admit right Reason's mastery over passion with these men who shrank not before the agonies of burning?

20 For even as towers on harbour-moles repulse the assaults of the waves and offer a calm entrance to those entering the haven, so the seven-towered right Reason of the youths defended the haven of righteousness and repulsed the tempestuousness of the passions.

21 They formed a holy choir of righteousness as they cheered one another on, saying:

22 'Let us die like brothers, O brethren, for the Law.

23 Let us imitate the Three Children at the Assyrian court who despised this same ordeal of the furnace.

24 Let us not turn cravens before the proof of righteousness.'

25 And one said, 'Brother, be of good cheer,' and another, 'Bear it out nobly'; and another recalling the past, 'Remember of what stock ye are, and at whose fatherly hand Isaac for righteousness' sake yielded himself to be a sacrifice.'

26 And each and all of them together, looking at each other brightly and very boldly, said, 'With a whole heart will we consecrate ourselves unto God who gave us our souls, and let us lend our bodies to the keeping of the Law.

27 Let us not fear him who thinketh he kills; for a great struggle and peril of the soul awaits in eternal torment those who transgress the ordinance of God.

28 Let us then arm ourselves with divine Reason's mastery of the passions.

29 After this our passion, Abraham, Isaac, and Jacob shall receive us, and all our forefathers shall praise us.'

30 And to each separate one of the brothers, as they were dragged off, those whose turn was yet to come said, 'Do not disgrace us, brother, nor be false to our brethren already dead.'

31 You are not ignorant of the love of brethren, whereof the divine and all-wise Providence has given an inheritance to those who are begotten though their fathers, implanting it in them even through the mother's womb; wherein brethren do dwell the like period, and take their form during the same time, and are nourished from the same blood, and are quickened with the same soul, and are brought into the world after the same space, and they draw milk from the same founts, whereby their fraternal souls are nursed together in arms at the breast; and they are knit yet closer through a common nurture and daily companionship and other education, and through our discipline under the Law of God.

32 The feeling of brotherly love being thus naturally strong, the seven brethren had their mutual concord made yet stronger. For trained in the same Law, and disciplined in the same virtues, and brought up together in the upright life, they loved one another the more abundantly. Their common zeal for moral beauty and goodness heightened their mutual concord, for in conjunction with their piety it rendered their brotherly love more fervent.

33 But though nature, companionship, and their virtuous disposition increased the ardour of their brotherly love, nevertheless the surviving sons through their religion supported the sight of their brethren, who were on the rack, being tortured to death; nay more,

they even encouraged them to face the agony, so as not only to despise their own tortures, but also to conquer their passion of brotherly affection for their brethren.

34 O Reasoning minds, more kingly than kings, than freemen more free, of the harmony of the seven brethren, holy and well attuned to the keynote of piety!

35 None of the seven youths turned coward, none shrunk in the face of death, but all hastened to the death by torture as if running the road to immortality.

36 For as hands and feet move in harmony with the promptings of the soul, so those holy youths, as if prompted by the immortal soul of religion, went in harmony to death for its sake.

37 O all-holy sevenfold companionship of brethren in harmony!

38 For as the seven days of the creation of the world do enring religion, so did the youths choir-like enring their sevenfold companionship, and made the terror of the tortures of no account.

39 We now shudder when we hear of the suffering of those youths; but they, not only seeing it with their eyes, nor merely hearing the spoken, imminent threat, but actually feeling the pang, endured it through; and that in the torture by fire, than which what greater agony can be found?

40 For sharp and stringent is the power of fire, and swiftly did it bring their bodies to dissolution.

41 And think it not wonderful if with those men Reason triumphed over the tortures, when even a woman's soul despised a yet greater diversity of pains; for the mother of the seven youths endured the torments inflicted on each several one of her children.

42 But consider how manifold are the yearnings of a mother's heart, so that her feeling for her offspring becomes the centre of her whole world; and indeed, here, even the irrational animals have for their young an affection and love similar to men's.

43 For example, among the birds, the tame ones sheltering under our roofs defend their nestlings; and those that nest upon the mountain tops, and in the rock clefts, and in the holes of trees, and in the branches, and hatch their young there, do also drive away the intruder.

44 And then, if they be unable to drive him away, they flutter around the nestlings in a passion of love, calling to them in their own speech, and they give succour to their young ones in whatever fashion they can.

45 And what need have we of examples of the love of offspring among irrational animals, when even the bees, about the season of the making of the comb, fend off intruders, and stab with their sting, as with a sword, those who approach their brood, and do battle against them even to the death?

46 But she, the mother of those young men, with a soul like Abraham, was not moved from her purpose by her affection for her children.

CHAPTER VII

A comparison of a mother's and father's affections, in this chapter are some mountain peaks of eloquence.

REASON of the sons, lord over the passions! O religion, that wast dearer to the mother than her children!

2 The mother, having two choices before her, religion and the present saving alive of her seven sons according to the tyrant's promise, loved rather religion, which saveth unto eternal life according to God.

3 O how may I express the passionate love of parents for children? We stamp a marvellous likeness of our soul and of our shape on the tender nature of the child, and most of all through the mother's sympathy with her children being deeper than the father's.

4 For women are softer of soul than men, and the more children they bear the more do they abound in love for them.

5 But, of all mothers, she of the seven sons abounded in love beyond the rest, seeing that, having in seven child-bearings felt maternal tenderness for the fruit of her womb, and having been constrained because of the many pangs in which she bore each to a close affection, she nevertheless through the fear of God rejected the present safety of her children.

6 Ay, and more than that, through the moral beauty and goodness of her sons and their obedience to the Law, her maternal love for them was made stronger.

7 For they were just, and temperate, and brave and great-souled, and lovers of each other and of their mother in such manner that they obeyed her in the keeping of the Law even unto death.

8 But nevertheless, though she had so many temptations to yield to her maternal instincts, in no single instance did the dreadful variety of tortures have power to alter her Reason; but the mother urged each son separately, and all together, to die for their religion.

9 O holy nature, and parental love, and yearning of parents for offspring, and wages of nursing, and unconquerable affection of mothers!

10 The mother, seeing them one by one racked and burned, remained unshaken in soul for religion's sake.

11 She saw the flesh of her sons being consumed in the fire, and the extremities of their hands and feet scattered on the ground, and the flesh-covering, torn off from their heads right to their cheeks, strewn about like masks.

12 O mother, who now knew sharper pangs than the pangs of labour! O woman, alone among women, the fruit of whose womb was perfect religion!

13 Thy firstborn, giving up the ghost, did not alter thy resolution, nor thy second, looking with eyes of pity on thee under his tortures, nor thy third, breathing out his spirit.

14 Neither didst thou weep when thou beheldest the eyes of each amid the torments looking boldly on the same anguish, and sawest in their quivering nostrils the signs of approaching death.

15 When thou sawest the flesh of one son being severed after the flesh of another, and hand after hand being cut off, and head after head being flayed, and corpse cast upon corpse, and the place crowded with spectators on account of the tortures of thy children, thou sheddest not a tear.

16 Not the melodies of the sirens nor the songs of swans with sweet sound do so charm the hearer's ears, as sounded the voices of the sons, speaking to the mother from amid the torments.

17 How many and how great were the tortures with which the mother was tormented while her sons were being tortured with torments of rack and fire!

18 But Inspired Reason lent her heart a man's strength under her passion of suffering, and exalted her to make no account of the present yearnings of mother-love.

19 And although she saw the destruction of her seven children and the many and varied forms of their torments, the noble mother willingly surrendered them through faith in God.

20 For she beheld in her own mind, even as it had been cunning advocates in a council-chamber, nature, and parenthood, and mother-love, and her children on the rack, and it was as if she, the mother, having the choice between two votes in the case of her children, one for their death and one to save them alive, thereupon regarded not the saving of her seven sons for a little time, but, as a true daughter of Abraham, called to mind his God-fearing courage.

21 O mother of the race, vindicator of our Law, defender of our religion, and winner of the prize in the struggle within thyself!

22 O woman, nobler to resist than men, and braver than warriors to endure!

23 For as the Ark of Noah, with the whole living world for her burden in the world-whelming Deluge, did withstand the mighty surges, so thou, the keeper of the Law, beaten upon every side by the surging waves of the passions, and strained as with strong blasts

by the tortures of thy sons, didst nobly weather the storms that assailed thee for religion's sake.

24 Thus then, if one both a woman and advanced in years, and the mother of seven sons, endured the sight of her children being tortured to death, the Inspired Reason must confessedly be supreme ruler over the passions.

25 I have proved, accordingly, that not only have men triumphed over their sufferings, but that a woman also has despised the most dreadful tortures.

26 And not so fierce were the lions around Daniel, not so hot was the burning fiery furnace of Mishael, as burned in her the instinct of motherhood at the sight of her seven sons being tortured.

27 But by her religion-guided Reason the mother quenched her passions, many and strong as they were.

28 For there is this also to consider, that had the woman been weak of spirit, despite her motherhood, she might have wept over them, and perchance spoken thus:

29 'Ah, thrice wretched me, and more than thrice wretched! Seven children have I borne and am left childless!

30 In vain was I seven times with child, and to no profit was my ten months' burden seven times borne, and fruitless have been my nursings, and sorrowful my sucklings.

31 In vain for you, O my sons, did I endure the many pangs of labour, and the more difficult cares of your upbringing.

32 Alas, for my sons, that some were yet unwed, and those that were wedded had begotten no children; I shall never see children of yours, nor shall I be called by the name of grandparent.

33 Ah me, that had many beautiful children, and am a widow and desolate in my woe! Neither will there be any son to bury me when I am dead!'

34 But the holy and God-fearing mother wailed not with this lamentation over any one of them, neither besought she any to escape death, nor lamented over them as dying men; but, as though she had a soul of adamant and were bringing forth the number of her sons, for a second time, into immortal life, she besought rather and entreated of them that they should die for religion's sake.

35 O mother, warrior of God in the cause of religion, old and a woman, thou didst both defeat the tyrant by thy endurance, and wast found stronger than a man, in deeds as well as words.

36 For verily when thou wast put in bonds with thy sons, thou stoodest there seeing Eleazar being tortured, and thou spakest to thy sons in the Hebrew tongue:

37 'My sons, noble is the fight; and do ye, being called thereto to bear witness for our nation, fight therein zealously on behalf of the Law of our fathers.

38 For it would be shameful if, while this aged man endured the agony for religion's sake, you that are young men shrank before the pain.

39 Remember that for the sake of God ye have come into the world, and have enjoyed life, and that therefore ye owe it to God to endure all pain for his sake; for whom also our father Abraham made haste to sacrifice his son Isaac, the ancestor of our nation; and Isaac, seeing his father's hand lifting the knife against him, did not shrink.

40 And Daniel, the just man, was cast to the lions, and Ananias, Azarias, and Mishael were flung into the furnace of fire, and they endured for God's sake.

41 And ye also, having the same faith unto God, be not troubled; for it were against Reason that ye, knowing righteousness, should not withstand the pains.'

42 With these words the mother of the seven encouraged every single one of her sons to die rather than transgress the ordinance of God; they themselves also knowing well that men dying for God live unto God, as live Abraham, and Isaac, and Jacob, and all the patriarchs.

CHAPTER VIII

The famous "Athletes of Righteousness." Here ends the story of courage called the Fourth Book of Maccabees.

SOME of the guards declared that when she also was about to be seized and put to death, she cast herself on the pyre in order that no man might touch her body.

2 O mother, that together with thy seven sons didst break the tyrant's force, and bring to nought his evil devices, and gavest an example of the nobleness of faith.

3 Thou wert nobly set as a roof upon thy sons as pillars, and the earthquake of the torments shook thee not at all.

4 Rejoice therefore, pure-souled mother, having the hope of thy endurance certain at the hand of God.

5 Not so majestic stands the moon amid the stars in heaven as thou, having lit the path of thy seven starlike sons unto righteousness, standest in honour with God; and thou art set in heaven with them.

6 For thy child-bearing was from the son of Abraham.

7 And had it been lawful for us to paint, as might some artist, the tale of thy piety, would not the spectators have shuddered at the mother of seven sons suffering for righteousness' sake multitudinous tortures even unto death?

8 And indeed it were fitting to inscribe these words over their resting-place, speaking for a memorial to future generations of our people:

HERE LIE AN AGED PRIEST
AND A WOMAN FULL OF YEARS
AND HER SEVEN SONS
THROUGH THE VIOLENCE OF A TYRANT
DESIRING TO DESTROY THE HEBREW NATION.
THEY VINDICATED THE RIGHTS OF OUR PEOPLE
LOOKING UNTO GOD AND ENDURING
THE TORMENTS EVEN UNTO
DEATH.

9 For truly it was a holy war which was fought by them. For on that day virtue, proving them through endurance, set before them the prize of victory in incorruption in everlasting life.

10 But the first in the fight was Eleazar, and the mother of the seven sons played her part, and the brethren fought.

11 The tyrant was their adversary and the world and the life of man were the spectators.

12 And righteousness won the victor and gave the crown to her athletes. Who but wondered at the athletes of the true Law?

13 Who were not amazed at them? The tyrant himself and his whole council admired their endurance, whereby they now do both Stand beside the throne of God and live the blessed age.

14 For Moses says, 'All also who have sanctified themselves are under thy hands.'

15 And these men, therefore, having sanctified themselves for God's sake, not only have received this honour, but also the honour that through them the enemy had no more power over our people, and the tyrant suffered punishment, and our country was purified, they having as it were become a ransom for our nation's sin; and through the blood of these righteous men and the propitiation of their death, the divine Providence delivered Israel that before was evil entreated.

16 For when the tyrant Antiochus saw the heroism of their virtue, and their endurance under the tortures, he publicly held up their endurance to his soldiers as an example; and he thus inspired his men with a sense of honour and heroism on the field of battle and in the labours of besieging, so that he plundered and overthrew all his enemies.

17 O Israelites, children born of the seed of Abraham, obey this Law, and be righteous in all ways, recognizing that Inspired Reason is lord over the passions, and over pains, not only from within, but from without ourselves; by which means those men, delivering up their bodies to the torture for righteousness' sake, not only won the admiration of mankind, but were deemed worthy of a divine inheritance.

18 And through them the nation obtained peace and restoring the observance of the Law in our country hath captured the city from the enemy.

19 And vengeance hath pursued the tyrant Antiochus upon earth, and in death he suffers punishment.

20 For when he failed utterly to constrain the people of Jerusalem to live like Gentiles and abandon the customs of our fathers, he thereupon left Jerusalem and marched away against the Persians.

21 Now these are the words that the mother of the seven sons, the righteous woman, spake to her children:

22 'I was a pure maiden, and I strayed not from my father's house, and I kept guard over the rib that was builded into Eve.

23 No seducer of the desert, no deceiver in the field, corrupted me; nor did the false, beguiling Serpent sully the purity of my maidenhood; I lived with my husband all the days of my youth; but when these my sons were grown up, their father died.

24 Happy was he; for he lived a life blessed with children, and he never knew the pain of their loss.

25 Who, while he was yet with us, taught you the Law and the prophets. He read to us of Abel who was slain by Cain, and of Isaac who was offered as a burnt-offering, and of Joseph in the prison.

26 And he spake to us of Phineas, the zealous priest, and he taught you the song of Ananias, Azarias, and Mishael in the fire.

27 And he glorified also Daniel in the den of lions, and blessed him; and he called to your minds the saying of Isaiah,

28 "Yea even though thou pass through the fire, the flame shall not hurt thee."

29 He sang to us the words of David the psalmist, "Many are the afflictions of the just."

30 He quoted to us the proverb of Solomon, "He is a tree of life to all them that do his will."

31 He confirmed the words of Ezekiel, "Shall these dry bones live?" For he forgat not the song that Moses taught, which teaches, "I will slay and I will make alive. This is your life and the blessedness of your days.'"

32 Ah, cruel was the day, and yet not cruel, when the cruel tyrant of the Greeks set the fire blazing for his barbarous braziers, and with his passions boiling brought to the catapult and back again to his tortures the seven sons of the daughter of Abraham, and blinded the eyeballs of their eyes, and cut out their tongues, and slew them with many kinds of torment.

33 For which cause the judgement of God pursued, and shall pursue, the accursed wretch.

34 But the sons of Abraham, with their victorious mother, are gathered together unto the place of their ancestors, having received pure and immortal souls from God, to whom be glory for ever and ever.

www.ingramcontent.com/pod-product-compliance
Lightning Source LLC
LaVergne TN
LVHW050945080826
845145LV00004B/1414

* 9 7 8 1 6 3 1 1 8 5 6 2 5 *